The First Book of Tasteless Fortune Cookie Fortunes

By
Joe Wang

Private Garden Press
Carlsbad, California

Private Garden Press
5067 Ciardi Court
Carlsbad, CA 92008

Wang, Joe
      The First Book of Tasteless Fortune Cookie Fortunes / Joe Wang

ISBN 978-0976630807

1. Humor   I. Title

9 8 7 6 5 4 3 2 1

"Joe Wang worked for 36 years writing fortunes for fortune cookies. He saved the ones that were rejected as being "tasteless." In this book you will find some of the worst and funniest of the rejected fortunes." - I. Kidding

"Joe Wang is a wickedly sick man." - Name withheld

"So funny and yet not funny at all. I guess it depends on how paranoid you are." - Harry Wun

Joe's Favorite Chinese Proverbs

A book is like a garden carried in the pocket.

A smile will gain you ten more years of life.

After three days without reading, talk becomes flavorless.

A Jade stone is useless before it is processed; a man is good-for-nothing until he is educated.

The longer the night lasts, the more our dreams will be.

There are always ears on the other side of the wall.

Dismantle the bridge shortly after crossing it.

Of all the stratagems, to know when to quit is the best.

To my wife, for not turning me in.

- Joe

6

Introduction

Most Distinguished Reader,

Hello. My name is Joe Wang. For thirty-six years I worked at a famous Chinese fortune cookie manufacturing company. You see, I was one of the people who wrote fortunes, like the ones you get in cookies at Chinese food restaurants.

As you may already know, Chinese fortune cookies aren't even Chinese at all. They were invented in America! Chinese fortune cookies were first served in California at the Japanese Tea Garden in San Francisco's Golden Gate Park in 1914 by a man named Makoto Hagiwara. (Of course, like everything else, a lot of Chinese fortune cookies are now made in China.)

At our company, before any fortune went into a cookie, it had to be approved by a committee of managers - the Fortune Approval Committee. Once a fortune was approved, it was mass produced and included in the next batch of cookies. Over the years, for various reasons, the Fortune Approval Committee rejected certain fortunes. These did NOT get printed and NEVER appeared in fortune cookies. Secretly, I collected these fortunes that the Fortune Approval Committee did not approve. This book is a collection of those fortunes that the Fortune Approval Committee rejected as "Tasteless."

The Fortune Approval Committee defined "Tasteless" as something that is offensive, tactless, insensitive or just plain vulgar.

Of course, "Tasteless" can also mean bland, as in boring, dull or uninspiring, which, in my most humble opinion, describes a lot of the fortunes you find these days in Chinese fortune cookies. For those of you who were expecting this book to be about bland cookies, I offer my sincerest apologies.

Just before you open a fortune cookie can be an anxious moment. This is especially true if you arc dining with other people, as it is customary to share your fortune with them by reading it aloud.

Thus, as you break open the cookie, you may be thinking something like, 'Will this fortune really come true?' or 'Will it change the direction of my life?' Or 'Will I be able to read this aloud without stumbling over the words?'

Some people attempt to deal with their anxiety with a little humor, such as committing everyone in the group to saying aloud the words "in bed" or "between the sheets," at the end of each fortune, as in "You will find great joy and happiness ... between the sheets!" With the "Tasteless" fortunes in this book, you don't need to do that... unless you want to.

May I recommend that as you read this book, you imagine yourself at a Chinese restaurant celebrating the birthday of someone you really just don't like — perhaps your boss or your least favorite relative.

May you always find good fortunes in your life.

Most humbly,

Joe Wang

Table of Contents

General

You will never know what hit you.

—— ——

Worse things are yet to come.

—— ——

Indigestion will wear your esophagus lining
down to nothing.

They are out to get you,
and they will succeed.

~~~~

When the larva hatches, it will become
infectious.

~~~~

Fear is only the beginning.

No matter how hard you try, it won't work.
Ever.

From now on out, it's hopeless.

Your dimmest moment is just about here.

Losing your mind will make the phantom limb syndrome go away.

<& <& <&

The last thing you see will be this fortune.

<& <& <&

Look up. The vultures are circling.

Your next trip will be your last

Look over your shoulder.

He won't go easy on you this time.

That isn't heartburn.

*

From here on out, the labor pains will seem
like a walk in the park.

*

Your darkest secret will be made known to
the one it will hurt the most.

It's really a cubic zirconium.

Prepare tonight for your worst nightmare
yet.

MENU

... ...

... ...

... ...

... ...

NO MSG

Of course, it's loaded with MSG, no matter
what the menu says.

Giving up is not just an option,
it's the only option.

You should have used the chopsticks.

Sitting with your back against the wall
would have been smarter.

The least of your worries will be that rash.

Don't drink the water here.

Patting a fat Buddha statue before you leave is essential for your continued health.

Be certain you know where the
exit signs are.

" " "

Look under your car
before starting it again.

" " "

They know, and they know
you don't.

Everyone else will be happy.

You will hear it coming.

You are being followed.

Love & Marriage

Your one chance for true love
came and went.

>>>>>

If it comes down to love or money, take
the money.

>>>>>

The problems in your marriage wall be
caused by your best friend.

The divorce proceedings will last longer
than the marriage.

> The lipstick on your collar
> will be the wrong color.

Your spouse already knows.

That which you admire the most about yourself will wrinkle and shrivel.

You will meet your soul mate too late.

This marriage won't be your last.

Your one true love
will show up too late.

†††

A new lover will enter your life, but turn
out to be already married.

†††

That prenuptial agreement
will really pay off.

Love will always be just a four letter word
for you.

(Not that four letter word.)

(Yes, that's the one.)

You will finally learn to be a great lover just before impotence sets in.

+ + +

Your alimony payments will get bigger after your next marriage ends.

+ + +

You will eventually get used to your spouse's cross-dressing.

The ecstasy will be followed by severe flatulence.

Everyone will know about your hot flashes.

Your spouse will leave you for a same-sex relationship

Your date will abandon you
in the desert.

‡ ‡ ‡

You will not attend your
spouse's funeral.

‡ ‡ ‡

Your lover will forget your birthday and
your anniversary.

You will lose your ring just
before the end comes.

A process server has papers
with your name on them.

You have already had your last kiss.

Your partner will passionately call out someone else's name.

" " "

Your spouse will collect double indemnity.

" " "

After the lightning strikes, not even professional counseling will help.

The cure will involve an implant.

_> <_

Your partner will develop a fascination with
whips and leather.

It will be something a bit
worse than herpes.

Money

You will not die cold and penniless, just penniless.

¥¥¥¥

Your accountant has some bad news for you.

¥¥¥¥

When your ship finally comes in, it will be a dinghy.

The next bear market will suck the last
ounce of life out of your retirement savings.

"">>>>>>>

Bankruptcy will be your best option.

"">>>>>>>

You will be the first in your family
to be truly poor.

Financial stress will cause your first round
of ulcers.

The bank ATM will shred your
next bonus check deposit.

Each new business venture you try
will fail miserably.

Your business partner will cheat you out of your last dollar.

Your checking account won't balance and you will never know why.

Your lotto numbers will be picked over and over on the days you don't buy a ticket.

The restaurant will refuse
your credit card.

$$$$

The magnetic strips on your credit cards
will all cease working at once.

$$$$

You will leave your wallet in the restaurant
and the waiter will have a great time
in Las Vegas before you find out.

You will eventually hear people say
behind your back "There, but for the
grace of God, go I."

● + ●

The money in your wallet is actually
counterfeit

● + ●

Identity fraud will cost you
thousands this year.

An IRS agent will call you soon.

* * * *

The only thing you will ever inherit is indebtedness.

* * * *

Your 40IK account will be rolled over into the gutter.

Everything you paid into social security will be given to someone else.

————— —————

After the hospital stay, you will never know financial security again.

————— —————

Bill collectors will hound you incessantly.

Your attorney will get
everything you own.

They will break into your car, take the
remote, open the garage door, and empty
the house.

Nothing wall be left.

You will soon discover just how
underinsured you really are.

The last thing they will take
will he your self-respect.

The loan officer will laugh
in your face.

The car valet is making copies of all your keys.

Your credit score will become a two digit number.

You will not have enough to pay the ransom.

Home and Family

You will find out the child wasn't really
yours after all.

^ ^ ^

There are things in your attic which will
scare someone to death.

^ ^ ^

Your sister will marry an ex-convict.

Your sister will become
an ex-convict.

The fire will start downstairs.

Your real biological parents
will finally come forward.

Your telephone number will
appear in Telemarketers Weekly
as the "Pick of the Week."

Your dentist will choose the
long needle.

Something dead is under your house.

After it happens, children will cringe
when they hear your name.

†††

Your family vacation will be postponed
until after you recover.

†††

An organ donor will be found for you.

Your next door neighbor is
watching you for a reason.

Those tree roots are wrapped
around more than your sewer line.

There will be news about
your condition soon.

The sprinklers will come on just after they finish toilet papering your house.

Your in-laws will move in permanently.

The home owners' association will try everything it can to get you to move.

You will only be left with a right eye.

• • •

**The hose to the washing machine will
break and your downstairs will be
flooded.**

• • •

Someone will come to haunt your house.

Your mother-in-law will join
a religious sect and call you daily
trying to convert you.

Your mother-in-law will have
your number on speed dial.

Your mother-in-law will remarry into
your side of the family.

The Peking duck will cause your gout
to flare up.

The swelling will leave stretch marks.

Only a few neighbors will be left after
the tornado.

Your next vacation will be remembered mostly for the time spent suffering from food poisoning.

** ** **

Your family will have to come up with the bail money.

** ** **

Your name will accidentally show up on the list of registered sex offenders.

You will spend the night in jail for a crime you did not commit.

Your pastor will be defrocked.

The results of the colonoscopy will be negative.

Your Health

The ambulance ride will be bumpy.

• • •

See your lawyer about making or updating your will.

• • •

You won't be able to scratch the itch.

The vims will mutate.

<***>

There will be no known antidote.

<***>

The cure will be worse than the disease.

You will not endure the pain.

§§§

It's just too late.

§§§

It will spread over your entire body.

You won't feel a thing.

† • †

Your doctor will recommend
you see a specialist.

† • †

The specialist won't have a
clue what to do.

It won't be covered by insurance.

You will go blind just after
learning sign language.

Your cold won't go away.

It will be a blood clot.

The pain will never go away.

Your cholesterol level won't matter.

The diagnosis will be alarming.

++++

The doctors will give up.

++++

The parasites will multiply.

You will have to sue your physician for malpractice.

‡‡‡

The scar from the surgery will be long and wide.

‡‡‡

You will know excruciating pain.

The pain from the root canal
will linger.

You should have flossed.

The anesthesia will wear off
too soon.

You'll be in traction before they put on the body cast.

The fever will break when the vomiting stops.

>>>>

To survive it, you will need a miracle.

The infection will spread.

Orientation will be difficult.

Changing positions won't help.

Pets & Animals

Your pet will soon run away. Forever.

_●__●_

A new veterinary bill will arrive soon.

_●__●_

Just before your next hot date, you will step
in dog doo-doo.

Even though you wash your shoes,
the smell of the dog doo-doo just won't go
away.

% % %

You will suddenly become allergic to your
favorite pet.

% % %

You will encounter a wild animal loose at
the zoo.

When you see the wild animal, you will urinate on yourself.

☼ ☼ ☼

Everyone at the zoo will see the stains on your pants.

☼ ☼ ☼

The stains on your pants won't come out.

Your cat will have lice and you won't find
out until it's too late.

**You will finally discover that your
cat actually doesn't like you.**

Your dog will bite your best friend.

Your best friend's dog will bite you.

Your best friend will bite your dog.

You will bite your best friend
and his dog.

Your cat will have only eight lives.

**A wild bird will nest in your house.
(Yes, inside.)**

Your cat will eat the wild bird that nested in
your house.

Your cat will die from eating the wild bird.

** **

The de-wormer won't work this time.

** **

**Your dog will be very healthy, except for
all the fleas.**

A lot of fleas.

Thousands and thousands of fleas.

OK... millions of fleas!

Your house will become infested
with mice.

Buying a snake and letting him loose at
night will take care of your mice problem.

Those aren't mice you hear at night.

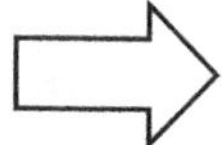

Rats.

Your snake will wander into your
neighbor's sewer pipes.

The snake bite venom will make your leg
really swell up.

You will be happy you fell into the elephant
dung.

A swarm of bees will invade
your porch.

The skunk odor won't come off you for
weeks.

<u>Work</u>

The recognition you deserve will be given
to someone else.

Your computer will soon manifest the most
interesting virus.

Your most trusted co-workers will soon
turn you in.

The next time you are called into your
supervisor's office will be the last.

Your random drug test will
be positive.

Your bonus will be less
than the taxes you owe.

A good friend at work
will sabotage the project

? ? ?

The promotion you have been waiting for
will be given to someone else.

? ? ?

Months of hard work will be lost when
your computer crashes.

You will soon have the opportunity to look
for a new job.

% % %

You will get to know a worker's
compensation attorney very well.

% % %

That raise you have been hoping for?
Forget about it.

Your boss at work will invite everyone out
to lunch, except you.

Your best years of work are behind you.

During your next presentation, everything
that can go wrong will.

The great idea you have will be stolen by
your employer and you will get nothing
for it.

**You will be given the choice of being
transferred to Barstow, California
or Fargo, North Dakota.**

The sexual harassment allegation will be
made against you by someone you don't
even know.

Your assistant will be promoted to be your supervisor and get you back for everything.

§

Your company will be taken over and your job outsourced to an island in the Indian Ocean.

§

Your best friend at work will start dating your ex-spouse.

An embarrassing email will get sent to
everyone in your address book.

**Even the mail room kid will stop
talking to you.**

When you return from vacation, your
computer and phone will be disconnected.

A competitor will steal
all your customers.

They will find your documents
jammed in the copy machine.

Your next boss will be even worse.

Joe's Favorite Fortunes

The first symptom will be
your hair falling out.

** **

A toy on the stairs will be your downfall.

** **

Eventually, not even reading glasses will
help you.

Your dreams will come true, and so will your nightmares.

Trust no one.

You're still dreaming.

In the near future, you will be buried alive.

When you least expect it, that's
when it will explode.

At least your wheelchair will be battery-
powered.

Seeing your doctor soon would be a good idea. And be sure to walk - don't run.

• • • •

A gold crown is in your future, courtesy of your dentist.

• • • •

Your last years will be spent with a bag. No, not a golf bag.

It's pointed at you right now.

The tumor is growing.

Your secret admirer will have split ends,
acne, and an overbite.

You will win a medal in a competition for
bi-lateral amputees.

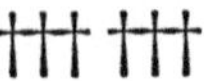

Your best invention will be illegal.

You will not hear the train
before it hits you.

Your enemies will know all about it.

The humiliation you will endure would repulse even the guards of Abu Ghraib.

Your good luck is about to run out.

The end will be a relief.

• • ••

No one will come to your party.

• • • •

You will miss out again.

You will be embarrassed
and no one will applaud.

Your golden parachute
will fail to open.

At the end of the rainbow will be absolutely
nothing.

This fortune belongs to someone else.
You took the wrong cookie.
A thousand days of bad luck will follow.

The only thing you will feel
will be the cold catheter.

You will be struck down by space junk.

You will be left out of the will and inherit
nothing at all.

From your cell, you will be able to see the
exercise yard.

You will die and no one will notice.

The ringing in your ears will only get
louder and louder.

Your fear of drowning will be justified.

Your children will always like their other
parent more than you.

The ants are coming.

... ...

Your license will be revoked.

... ...

Deep, dark depression is just around
the corner.

Your <u>last</u> birthday will be spent alone.

You will have to tunnel out

All your friends will conspire
against you.

Your next fortune cookie will be empty.

⧈

Thousands will try before you, and you will
fail too.

⧈

When you look inside, it will be outside.
When you look outside, it will be inside.

You will be wrong, and
everyone will know it but you.

The grief counseling will be useless.

Fungus will grow in your navel.

By the time you get there,
they will all be gone.

§§§

Don't eat the cookie.

§§§

This is as good as it gets.

COMING SOON
FROM JOE WANG

THE SECOND BOOK OF TASTELESS
FORTUNE COOKIE FORTUNES

TASTELESS FORTUNE COOKIE
FORTUNES FOR KIDS

EVEN MORE (AND REALLY GROSS)
TASTELESS FORTUNE COOKIE
FORTUNES

Made in the USA
Monee, IL
07 July 2026